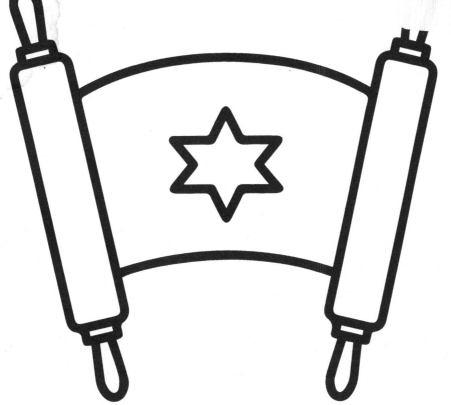

This Book Belogs To

_____

_____

_____

I SPY with my little eye someting beginning with......

A Is for

Afikomen

I SPY with my little eye someting beginning with......

B Is for

Barbecue

I SPY with my little eye someting beginning with......

C Is for

Cap

I SPY with my little eye someting beginning with......

D Is for

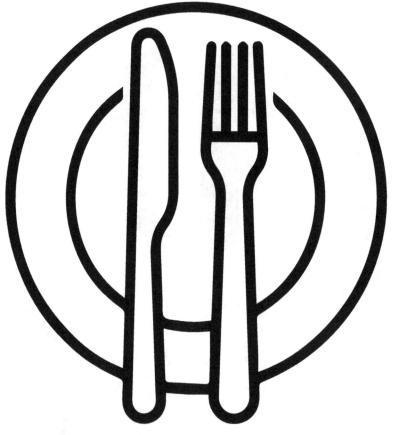

Dinner

I SPY with my little eye someting beginning with......

E Is for

Egyptian

I SPY with my little eye someting beginning with......

F

 Is for

Fish

I SPY with my little eye someting beginning with.......

G

G Is for

Grape

I SPY with my little eye someting beginning with......

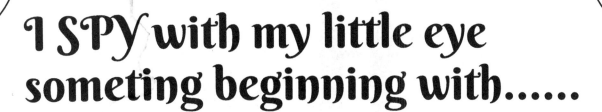

H Is for

Hamsa

I SPY with my little eye someting beginning with......

I Is for

Isis

I SPY with my little eye someting beginning with......

J Is for

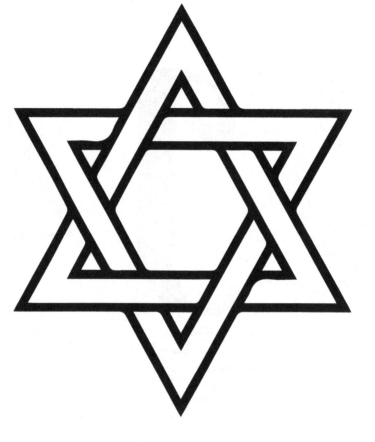

Judaism

I SPY with my little eye someting beginning with......

K Is for

King

I SPY with my little eye someting beginning with......

L Is for

Lamb

I SPY with my little eye someting beginning with......

M Is for

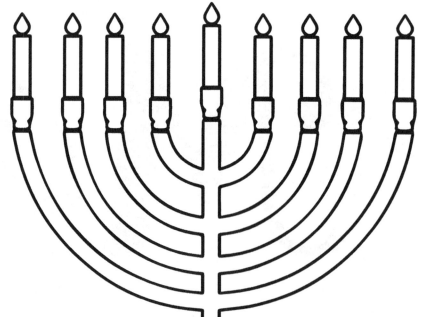

Menorah

I SPY with my little eye someting beginning with......

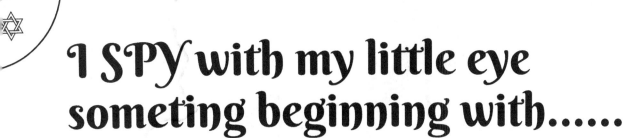

N Is for

Nosh

I SPY with my little eye someting beginning with......

O
Is for

Olive Oil

I SPY with my little eye someting beginning with......

P
Is for

Pharaoh

I SPY with my little eye someting beginning with......

Q

Q Is for

Quill

I SPY with my little eye someting beginning with......

R Is for

Rooster

I SPY with my little eye someting beginning with......

S Is for

Seder

I SPY with my little eye someting beginning with......

T Is for

Torah

I SPY with my little eye someting beginning with......

U

Umbrella

I SPY with my little eye someting beginning with......

V Is for

Vegetables

I SPY with my little eye someting beginning with......

W Is for

Wine

I SPY with my little eye someting beginning with......

X Is for

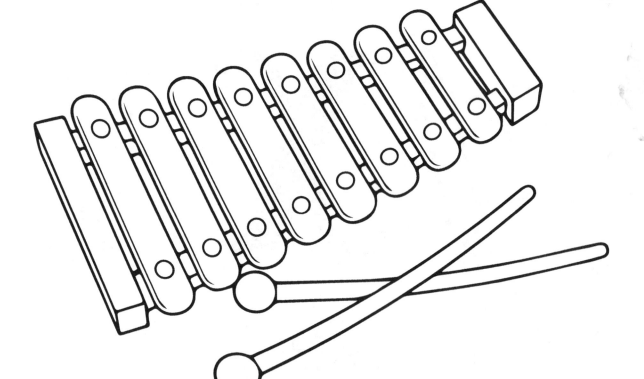

Xylophone

I SPY with my little eye someting beginning with......

Y Is for

Yom

I SPY with my little eye someting beginning with......

Z
Is for

Zakat

Made in United States
North Haven, CT
16 April 2022